Susan Abulhawa's beautifully crafted poems are written in the great lyric tradition of Pablo Neruda and Mahmoud Darwish, yet they possess their own striking originality. Their themes range widely across a terrain littered with Palestinian memories and torments, the tangled joys of love and loss, and pervading all, an embrace of life itself in all its wildness.

—RICHARD FALK
UN Special Rapporteur
on the situation in the
Occupied Palestinian Territories

Susan Abulhawa's poetry stems from the long-forgotten, dark, luminous, tightly knit root of flesh and soul. The figure of the Palestinian she carves from the bark of the olive trees of the troubled landscape of her memory is that of the oppressed, the violated, the exiled. But then, in her voice, suffering and exile only bring us closer to the intricate and true essence of life—and poetry: a relentless struggle for love, freedom, and dignity. Her flesh open, her soul open, Susan Abulhawa is able to capture in a handful of naked words the infinite anxiety, and the unaccomplished delight, of the wide human experience.

—AMIN KHAN
Poet, author of *Vision of the Return*

T0094707

Palestinian resistance has produced some of the most stunning poetry I've ever read, and Susan Abulhawa's *My Voice Sought the Wind* is exceptionally gripping and honest. Her verse can be blunt and potent, allowing us to peek into a world of defiance in the face of a million humiliations. And Abulhawa's words of loving warmth in spite of occupation's dehumanization are a kind of protest that gives me hope for us all.

—SHERRY WOLF
Author, public speaker
Editor, *International Socialist Review*

MY
VOICE
SOUGHT
THE
WIND

in loving memory of

Wanda Wentz,
"Mama Wandaful"
(October 28, 1946–June 11, 2013)

Yousef Raed Maree
(April 29, 1994–December 7, 2012)

Lamia Hijazi
(December 28, 1958–November 19, 2012)

Alexis Smith
(December 12, 1972–October 17, 2008)

Midnight
(February 2, 2008–November 8, 2010)

MY VOICE SOUGHT THE WIND

SUSAN ABULHAWA

JUST WORLD BOOKS

CHARLOTTESVILLE, VIRGINIA

**JUST
WORLD
BOOKS**

Just World Books is an imprint of Just World Publishing, LLC.

Typesetting by Jane T. Sickon for Just World Publishing, LLC.

Publisher's Cataloging-in-Publication

(Provided by Quality Books, Inc.)

Abulhawa, Susan.
    My voice sought the wind / by Susan Abulhawa.
    pages cm
    Poems.
    LCCN 2013948072
    ISBN 978-1-935982-32-6

    I. Title.

PS3601.B86M9 2013   811'.6
                    QBI13-600153

Mi voz buscaba el viento para tocar su oido
My voice sought the wind to touch your hearing

– Pablo Neruda

Contents

SUSAN ABULHAWA

ABOUT SUSAN ABULHAWA

Susan Abulhawa, a displaced Palestinian from Jerusalem, lives in Pennsylvania. Her debut novel, *Mornings in Jenin* (Bloomsbury, 2010), was an international bestseller, translated into thirty-two languages. She is a contributor to several anthologies, including *Searching Jenin* (Cune Press, 2003), and *Seeking Palestine: New Palestinian Writing on Exile and Home* (Interlink, 2013).

Susan is a human rights activist, political essayist, and frequent speaker on matters pertaining to the "Middle East". She is also the founder of Playgrounds for Palestine (www.playgroundsforpalestine.org), a non-governmental organization that upholds the Right to Play for Palestinian children.

Susan holds a graduate degree in biomedical science from the University of South Carolina School of Medicine. She is a signatory to and active participant in the Boycott, Divestment, and Sanctions (BDS) campaign, which calls for an economic and cultural boycott of Israel.

A NOTE, BEFORE
YOU READ ON...

I wrote poetry before I wrote anything else. Poems in Arabic, to be precise.

I wrote them as a child. They were sophomoric, I'm sure. And they're all long gone.

About a crush I had on our Iraqi neighbor, Kamal.

About Gadeer, the mean girl in first grade, who used to pull one of my pigtails down. I didn't know how to fix it and had to endure the day with lopsided hair.

About my first-grade Arabic teacher—I don't remember her name—who was so nice to me, and the bus driver who stopped to get me ice cream one day after dropping everyone else off. He told me I was very special. I told him he was special, too, and he smiled beautifully. At forty-three years old, I still remember his face and see the love that poured from his eyes, as if I reminded him of a daughter or granddaughter he had lost. I still think about him sometimes, because love is never forgotten.

I wrote poems about my Teta and my Uncle Jamal, with whom I shared a small room in Kuwait. Their snoring kept me up at night, until the day I found myself without them and could not fall asleep without their sleeping noises.

Then, long after I learned to sleep to silence, long after my exile brought me to foreignness in English, I woke up one day and understood that Arabic had been stolen from my tongue. Or maybe it ran away of its own accord, like a neglected child might do. I miss it terribly. I have phantom pains where those poems used to be, before they were amputated as I slept to silence.

I found new words to put to the language inside me, and I did it always in private and in secret. I only wrote when I was in love or in pain, which were often one and the same. This is a selection of poems that I created over the course of five years. I have decided to publish them, with gratitude to all the readers who have allowed me into their hearts and thoughts over the years.

Love,
susie

PALESTINIAN,
BLACK & BLUE

The Gift of Olive Oil

A token
Something from the soil of things shared
   a heritage
   a longing
   a wound
The sweet and bitter tastes of centuries gone
The hard caress of weatherworn hands of pickers
The tales of backbreaking toil,
   scribbled on beautiful *fellaheen* faces
The ballads of old, sung to trees
   and sleepless Palestinian children
The untamed agonies of loss and expired love

   the soot of memory,
   the breath of hope,
   the fury,
   the tears of babies
   and patriarchs,
   mothers and whores
   gods and men

This nectar of tragedy is ours to consume
Ours to bury and bring back to life

Take it from their tireless hands
Their boundless capacity to endure

And without bread or *za'atar*, dip your finger in this oil
Press it between your tongue and palate

Do it again

Until you hear the primal calls of an earth packed
    beneath boot steps and tank treads

And it will haunt you with an unexpected song

Black

June Jordan was born Black
And she was become Palestinian
Like my sister Suheir Hammad
I was born Palestinian
And I am become Black

But is that really so?
My hair is straight-ish
My skin is brown
My nose is big and long, crooked and pointy,
    and all kinds of fucked up
Still, I can access white privilege if I want

But that would be worse
Would rip my soul
So I search for the Black in me

I find it in the Ethiopian women
Enslaved by my Arab forefathers
Those women who lost their identities
Gave birth to Arab babies
And injected Afrika into my veins

I find it in
The white supremacy
That raped me

I find it where
A European took my grandma's house
Painted my country white
Kicked us out to the cold curb
Killed our neighbors
Cut my brother's balls off
Motherfuckers fucked my mother
Then dragged me by the hair
    and told me I needed liposuction
And a nose job

It is where I believed I was ugly
When I tried to be white
When I put down my flat bread and picked up a fork
And Mrs. Wall said I was "white enough" to
Stop being a "nigger-lover"

I find it where White boys dug up my ancestors' bones
Built a "Tolerance Museum" over their graves
Put on uniforms and held me at gunpoint
For a laugh
'Cause little white girls pushed
Me out of the pool one day
Screaming mean things at me in Hebrew

I feel it in the way
My Arab brethren
Considered me human ONLY
After I got a USA passport
Because, otherwise, I am vermin
That they can feel sorry for
And be outraged about
A thing
Fit for refugee camps that aren't fit for humans
And good for cheap labor
Or a cheap whore

I find it in the dictates that
I am the wrong kind of human

Because I'm Palestinian
And Jesus was Palestinian
And Jesus was Black

I find Black from
The poetry in my heart
The song on my lips
And music in my hips

I am Palestinian
And in the blue and bruise of my heart,
I am become Black
Because Black is beautiful
And the beautiful in me
Is Black

Ramadan in el Ghorba

All the restaurants are open
Taunting with various scents
Most don't even know it's Ramadan
Or that I'm fasting

There is no solidarity in *el ghorba*
Not from shopkeepers or neighbors

A single *fanoos* is nowhere to be found
You don't walk down the street here and
Nod to another in mutual acknowledgment
Of shared hunger and thirst

There will be no superhuman meal tonight
No gathering of first second and third
    generation cousins

There is no collective exhaustion here
Followed by collective merriment

There will be no sitting on the floor around the feast
The *adan* will not breeze through our hearts
    with its permission

Here, the time is different, too
And so I will not do the exact same thing
At the exact same time
As millions will do every evening this month

Dusk will come unannounced, like any other sundown
Someone recommended coffee instead of Zoloft
    to break the fast.
I'll do my best to stick with *shorabat freika*

And a pre-recorded *adan*

Mahmoud Darwish

We saw you tear off your limbs
To pass through the narrow passage

Now you know
Where birds fly after the last sky

What color is the last beat of a poet's heart?

What word is it?

Is it the humble majesty of the Holy Sepulcher?
Or the lullaby of the *adan* over Palestine?

What was that last contraction
That sent ripples of love and grief
    across our earth?

The last call from the Voice of Palestine.
You left us too soon, *ya* Mahmoud.

Mahmoud Darwish is a critically acclaimed literary rarity considered
one of the most important poets in the Arabic language. In his life, and
now in death, he is beloved by us all as the *Voice of Palestine*.

The Siege

Every night, hearts break and bleed themselves to sleep
And in the morning,
They are whole and full again

Suraya
Moves through the day gripping her poems
Holding her breath
With limbs that slowly become heavy
As the earth spins
The hours pass
The sky dims
And Gaza is still under siege.

She climbs into the trauma of enclosure
Tucks herself in
As darkness quietly curls her limbs
And she closes her eyes
So she can open them on the other side
Where her poetry assembles into dreams

Mjahid
Gazes westward
His eyes skimming the surface of the Mediterranean
An expanse hemmed in by
Mercenary ships and
An invisible three-mile radius

He turns eastward, then north
Where forever and futures bounce
Off metal and fences and meanness

Hope hunches in the southern corner
Battered, breathing in the dank and dark
Underworld of tunnels

He looks upward
And plays his oud to
Hang the stars back in place
After the sky has fallen

Laila and Yousef
Imagine an ephemeral
Salve of touch
As love's sorrowful hands
Burrow in the sand
To seek redemption
And a story unwritten begs
To breathe

They find their way to the shore
Eyes upon the same empty moon
And sky devoid of promise

The winds caress her cheeks
And, miles away, wrap around him
Until their fingers find each other
Inch closer
Interlace
And they hold hands

Across sky and wind and moon and miles

Sister Palestinian I

Sister Palestinian
Your fate was written

The day you played hopscotch
When they pulled the land from under your feet

So you carried your country on your back
In the bags handed to you on the long march
    to oblivion

When your father, king of his castle,
    was forced to sleep on dirt
You served him coffee and scrubbed his feet
    to save his pride

When your mother went mad and died with anguish
Your tears watered a refugee's garden

Someone put two gold bracelets on your wrist
The braided bangles we all wear
And you stared at them on your wedding night
As you gripped the bedposts with white knuckles

The first time your husband hit you
It nearly knocked the country off your back

But your first baby was a promise too precious
So you sewed Palestine to your skin

When he came back from Israel's prison
You tenderly dressed his wounds
Kissed them
And you prayed for him

You loved him
And he left five months
After your second daughter was born

European women, he said
Knew how to please a man
He said
You had never been an exciting fuck

He didn't mind that European women couldn't
Pronounce his name

He never knew about his third daughter
Whom you named Fairuz*
For the voice that was your only solace

When another of history's storms razed your house
The winds carried you to foreign lands

---

* Fairuz is a Lebanese singer whose rare voice is revered throughout the
Arab world and sounds, to me, like freedom.

And you were at home in the devastating
Freedom of answering to no one

When, then, you became an exciting fuck
You found yourself searching, over and over,
For some meaning in the heartbreak
Of an empty orgasm

The girls you raised were not Palestinian
The house you built was not yours
The country tethered to your skin sags
As if a body of sorrow

You deserve better, Sister
Come back in another life

To a country that holds you
A man who honors the language of your heart

And daughters who will sing
For you a Palestinian lullaby
Before you finally sleep

Sister Palestinian II

We swim on the surface of this frozen dream
passing one another, lost.

Beyond the cold crust lies
    a country siphoned from our veins
    where the hills of God are carved and paved
    and apartheid metastasizes into the *wadis*
    through the *sanasil* and precious groves.

I see you, clawing at the ice
    jabbing it with the jag of your broken bones
    with the aimless bullet of the son
    coaxing it with the heat of the dawn
    the wreckage of the day
    the silent despair of uprooted trees.

Might there be mercy for us?

Perchance ten more will not lose a limb today
Thousands will not leave school to scrounge for food.

Perchance Lena will marry, instead of
    committing suicide
And Ahmed will dream tonight, instead of shivering
    in his own piss.

I see you, Sister.

Your eyes make me despise the *ghorba* soaking my skin
    and I tear at my tongue to rip
    the English it planted
    in this manufactured fate.

I don't want this world of deceit and theft, Sister.

Sit with me on the floor of our damnation
I've made plates of *zeit* and *za'atar*
Eggs and fried tomatoes
And there is bread from the ruins of a *taboon*.

We can eat like the *fallahat* we are
    sing Palestine's ballads as death rolls
    shoots, marches, and flies through her.

Sit with me.

Let us eat and sing
    bear witness
    and love
    through this winter.

Wala

It's 3 am
In the cattle cage

The line is long
And thick
With bodies

You wait

A *jibneh* sandwich
With cucumber
In a plastic bag
Clutched in your callused laborer's hand

Your wife prepared your breakfast and lunch
She was up before you
And together you prayed a predawn *salat*

She kissed your face and said
Allah ma'ak ya habibi
Allah be with you, my love

You kiss the faces of your sleeping babies
You haven't seen them awake in months
And you wonder
Has Walid's voice begun to crack yet?
Have Wijdad's hips begun to flare?
How big was Suraya's smile when she came home
    with her report card?

It's 4 am
In the cattle cage

Still, you wait
The line before you is so long
And behind you now, it is longer

Few speak
You're packed so damn tight
That you hold one another upright

You see your own fatigue
Reflected in the weariness etched on
The faces all around you

You look away
Pine for a smoke
But who the hell can afford that?

You stare at the graffiti beyond the
Iron bars holding you in
Written just for you
Written
By zionist settlers sucking the breath from your lungs

You understand the meaning
Of their English words
"Die Sand Niggers"

Sometimes
You pine for that, too.

It's 5 am
In the cattle cage

The soldiers arrive
The line loosens
You take one step forward
Propelled by the weight of bodies
Behind you

Your *jibneh* sandwich
With cucumber
In a plastic bag
Is crushed.
It never survives

It's 7 am
In the cattle cage

Now is your turn
You produce your papers
Unfold and refold
Eyes down
Heart down
Your shoes are down on their luck

But
You're out of the line
Fifteen men before you were pulled aside
And you tried not to look
Not to hear the one begging
Don't hit me

It's 7:30 am
On the cattle bus

You ride
The country they stole from you
Seeds outside your window
And you imagine
The man you would have been
The man you should have been
Out there
Riding the family steed
The thoroughbred mares your grandfather
Raised and nurtured and loved
In a Palestine
Un-raped
Un-stolen

It's 8 am
You get off the cattle bus

Your crushed *jibneh* sandwich
With cucumber
In a plastic bag
In one hand

Your eyes down
Heart down
You put your toolbox down to knock
On the zionist settler's back door
Where the help goes

But

The zionist settler boss-man yells
Wala
Mish hon el yom!
Not there today
Boy!

And all you can do is thank Allah that your
Wife and your babies are not
There to hear them call you
Wala

Facts on the Ground

A column from my throat
Into my belly
Spins

The apparition of a future snuggles
In the space between my neck and clavicle

I tuck my fingers there to hold it in place
As I have done since memory

The desert sighs in my bed
Sleep seeps through a crack in my teacup

My Jiddo's farm got paved
And my Teta died in a bug-infested shack.

The violence of longing dances on my dreams
Desire lashing the back of the slave that I am

Europeans slept in Teta's Jerusalem bed.

The fortune teller finds you upside down
Paving a bypass road to a fate you promised yourself
Like the Jewish-only bypass roads to a
    divine real estate prize
To bypass me
To bypass Palestine and overlay perfectly chiseled stone

They cut their food with knifes and forks
    and drink their tea cold.

But trying a detour to destiny takes you somewhere else
Because my Teta's home wasn't built for Europeans
And my Jiddo's farm wasn't loved to be smothered
    by perfectly chiseled stone

They're shiny facts on the ground
Lies, psalms, and foreign fables planted
    and watered every day

We cut our food with bread and drink our tea hot,
    with fresh mint!

And you're still in me
As Palestine shall always be in, and of, me

The Seed After the Seed

I am the seed after the seed of that grandfather

That grandmother who

Herded their sheep and goats
In the sylvan mist of country

Through the stretch of the monotone of ballads
And on the small stitches of
Embroidered heritage

As they were being herded
To the precipice of history

Where the slave turned
Slaveowner
The victim became the
Victimizer

The home a prison
The goat a burden

And the cries of children drowned us all

I am the seed after the seed of that soldier

The boots with the laces past the ankles
The guns packed and carried

Loaded with fury and made-up stories
As he marched into that inferno

When they threw the *adan* from the window
And it tumbled down the mountain

Breaking our bones
Melting our eyes
And gouging our dreams

I am the seed of the seed of time

Of love and oblivion

I am you, my darling
I am the dirt in your heart

Samer Issawi:
For You, Jerusalem Son

Apartheid's outlaw
Has crooked white teeth
An Adam's apple and an angled jaw

A beautiful face
With a knowing smile, gentle eyes
And masculine grace

O native son, my brother

Your eyes have sunk in darkness's pain
Sleepless nights crawl on your skin
And daylight climbs the links of your rusty prison chain

Religion made a mistake
So your body shrinks
And shadows trample your ribs
While a thousand senators quake

In your hallowed belly, Jerusalem screams
Chokes on your mother's tears
And shakes these tired dreams

From your body's excavation of death
The ruin of nations is carved in your palm
And a sorrowful flag holds its breath

O native son, my brother

You carry your broken frame
Through the decay of health
And death hangs its head in shame

You are the prince
Where the jasmine sings
The bougainvillea prances
And the tyrants wince

Palestine rises on the days
They siphoned from your veins
As if crutches to steady her gait
For a gun can but power feign

O native son, my brother

Fly over this country your wish
And pour the *adan* from your wings
Let the church bells chime from your smile
And the walls fall by your kiss

Our tears will rain and the *wadis* flood
Until another thousand years
Have sunk in Jerusalem's mud

We will harvest the olives with your name
And your heart forever stake our claim

Awake on Memories
in Gaza

It is night
Darkness floats about
My heart thrashes
Beating against my chest
And I try to remember the terror
So I can remember how to calm it

Was it the spider web in the sky, the
White phosphorous death?
Or the sonic booms?

My eyes bulge
The better to see should
My heart break free
And make a run for it

Sitti's songs do not work tonight
What was that pretty girl's name?
The one who made my heart flutter?
I can't recall and a flutter is ridiculous now
With an explosion knocking on my life

That's it, it was the explosion!
Except it didn't tear at me
It was my friend, Sameer, whose body was torn
With his family

…and Sameera
That was her name!

I remember now, it was not me
My heart has calmed inside its cage
But I think it will never flutter again

Ground Zero Mosque

Fun
In the sun
In this City of One

It's Ramadan!

But who can tell?
Shout Rejoice!
The *adan* fell
And broke its voice

A young woman pulled her *hijab*
Uncovered her hair
She lowered her eyes
She said: "This isn't fair"
Surprise!

This is Ground Zero, baby
Hallowed rocks
A bar or brothel, maybe
But not
A
Mosque

LOVE AND NERUDA

Earth's First Story

Come with me, *habibi*
To this field of sky
That we made

Come see what I have planted
And what has blossomed since

The face at the airport
Has grown into an ocean
Wherein I happily drown in a fantasy
That crashes upon its pebbled shore

Carry me over a silent street
Through a moment of snow
To that impossible perfection
And stubborn splendor

The rain here
Will shower us with dreams
And the sun
Will show us things we've never seen

Come to this timeless place
Where lovers dare to love
And fear has no say

Right and wrong will hold hands
To make love and blend
Into a country beneath our feet

Swim into my flesh
And taste the fever that burns my body

Feel the tempest in my breasts
And kiss me

Let me drink from your river
And nestle my head on your belly

As we did once with
The sympathies of Adam and Eve
As if Earth's first story

Untitled and Unfinished

In a room of flags and books
The country in my blood
Reached across the ocean
To turn my head

When snow carpeted the streets
A fireplace lit my heart

And when the moon called
The ocean swept me away

There are a thousand ways to love
And I loved him ten thousand ways

Seasons of a Sapling

As it turned out
The fruit of an uprooted, discarded sapling
Was a winter flower, planted in a story

He found me in a book
I found him in my dreams
And we reached across skies

He beheld the petals, turned the pages
Thumb and index tasting the cries I always grip
Or was it something else?

One by one, he leafed them in his hands
As I counted he-loves-me-he-loves-me-nots

And with each new sun, with each new page
Winter gave way to a forbidden springtime garden
Wherein I held my breath, for the sheer beauty of it
My insolent heart stormed away and nestled
    in secret at his neck
Then taunted me with the mystery
Of what made it beat so fast, so vigorously

With the pleasures of his scent
The softness of his lips
The kindness in his eyes
The tenderness of his touch
With all the affairs of my longing

I'd follow if I could and rest my head there instead
I'd put my lips to his and close my eyes
And at the cusp of summer
We would know how truly gentle
Are these defiant hearts

Neruda in a Heart

Let your voice seek the wind, my love
I'll climb the air with my bare heart
And tug at God's cloak
Until I find the sound so loved
Hold it to touch my ear
And fill my empty womb

I'll stay a while
At *the edge of a story* that almost was
A relentless longing that is
And a country that forever shall be

Meet me there
In the rapture of freedom
The abandon of this determined love
And the expanse of what we found

Wrap me in your embrace and hold me there
To quiet this mad heart of mine
If but for a moment

I'll take it home, petulant and unruly thing
And sing for it a lullaby of your voice in the wind

For to quiet Neruda in a heart is also an offense

The Sound So Loved

Oh, Neruda
His voice still echoes in my heart
And I close my eyes
To let memory
Pour his laughter over my body

I try to grip his words
To pull him through
And bring his lips to touch my ear

You understand, I know
How the heart of a poet will break
But I try to keep it whole
Lest it cry or beat too hard
And drown the sound so loved

What I Did Today,
for Tomorrow

I peeled our shadows from the street
And made of them a dress
To wear to his birthday party

I found the moon in my chest
And went there to be alone

I don't oblige much anymore
Because I can't

But I'm not so foolish to think I truly can't
So today I summoned a few things

I climbed onto my name
And watched from afar, unseen

I closed my eyes
The better to see his face

His hands gripped my waist
And we kissed with that hunger
I've come to know

I tilted my head
Felt his lips on my neck

And I ached
A desperate and unforgiving
Ache

But I couldn't see anything more
I couldn't remember either

And I can't finish this poem

Save a Place for Me

In your heart
Save a place for me
A space and a time
One day, perhaps
Of five in May
Just for me
Just for you
An everland
Of truth still true
And love unrefined
Under the shade of dreams

In your heart
Save a place for me
A space and a time
A blink or a breath
Or a shy tilt of the head
Just for me
Just for you

HISTORY OF LOVE

The poem opposite refers to Layla of *Majnoun Layla*, the story of Qais and Layla, one of the greatest love stories ever told and one that inspired Shakespeare's *Romeo and Juliet*. It was derived from classical Arabic literature and later popularized by the twelfth-century Kurdish poet Nizami Ganjavi in his *Khamsa* collection of narrative poems. For the love of Layla, Qais's heart melted and drove him to madness—more so because he was refused her hand in marriage. He was found dead in the wilderness in 688 A.D. by a rock where he had carved his last verse of poetry for Layla. This tale of love has been passed through generations over many centuries. Some of the greatest, most sensual Arabic poetry was written or inspired by the depth of Qais's love and longing for Layla. Yet, in more than fourteen centuries, no one has seen Laila except as Qais saw her—the beautiful, unattainable essence of love, passion, and desire. Her suffering has always been eclipsed by his, and yet I think she did suffer. I think she loved him, too.

Qais, Your Layla Speaks

I

I know creation held its breath
When my eyes lay upon
Your gaze upon me

The moon sneaked
Away from night
And peeped behind the sun
To behold Love

I hear your sigh in the wind
I feel your eyes close in fantasy
I hear the heart that knows only me
Until I am drenched in all that is you

I am so far from where I am
My body, my voice, are not my own
Forgive me, our desert son
For my soul is always where you tread

I slip from my flesh
And wander Arabia
To gather the poetry
You plant in the sand

These desert flowers are all
That tether my heart to its own beat
That make my sun rise over the mountains
And give flavor its taste

Your love has woven through me
It owns and commands me
And injects your *junoun*, your madness
Into my nights

By day, I wear my face like a dress
With kohl I draw the beauty you've imparted to my eyes
And paint my lips
Perchance you'll divine their shape beneath this veil

I roam the *souq*
Under a scorpion of a sun
Heavy with the full
Weight of fate

When I lie in this bed
Crushed beneath false honor
Tangled in threads of rightness
And unnatural morality

It is you who swims through my body
And releases time from history

How I long for your wild heart
The yearning you cannot tame
Has made me ill
With rectitude

II

I called your name in my sleep
And awoke, startled by the clarity
Of this love

Like the small quiver of dew
In the stillness of morning's first light
My eyes raised their lids, lashes
Combing through the still air

I wrapped my arms around my body
Closed my waking eyes
Yanked at time to stretch a few more moments to dream
And I rolled my body into the ghost that is you

But you left with the night
And I must inhabit this light without you

I wash the sheets of my bed
And as I stretch my arms to hang them to dry
I yearn for a miracle to bring you running to me

But there are no miracles to be had
So I hang the next
Had they but been your stains
My love

III

Whose body is this that suffocates my heart?
Whose coarse hands are these that hold me?

I cannot own my hours
My days belong to this castle and these servants
And as I escape to you each night
He comes to me
I clench my fists, nails burrowing into my flesh

To stab these moments
I grip the pillows to hold your face steady
My eyes squeezed shut

IV

My heart burns for you
Even as my body
Turns to winter

Childbirth has thickened
My small waist
And kohl runs down my cheeks
Like black tears

My breasts cower—wilted flowers
Never knowing your touch
And my lips have paled
Unkissed by love

Propriety has seared
Through my sinful prayers
And left my flesh
Parched by decorum

I have waited eagerly for this decay
To be free
From the breath of this life
That keeps me from you

Will you still love me
Without a maiden's glory?
I am only woman, without raiment
Made of your poem's corpses

Meet me now, *habibi*
In this prairie
Where poetry blooms in the desert sand

I will wait with a heart
Oppressed by the wait
In that moment where we first met

I'll wait
With the anguish of a body untouched
A story untold

In the melancholy of a morning without dew
I am here, breathing your *junoun*

Hester Dearest

I dreamt of Hester last night
How the world was a darker place
   precisely for her beauty
Proud on a scaffold
An honorable man at her feet, peeking at her bosom

Do you feel victorious in your defeat, dearest Hester?

What is that absorbing their scorn?
Is it submission? Indifference?

Arthur was there
Did you know?
Did he tell you that honor is hollow without love?

Even the shinier it is polished
The more a spooned-out decay it makes of you

A reference to Nathaniel Hawthorne's *The Scarlet Letter*. Hester
Prynne is one of those literary characters who have stayed with me
over the years. I am interested in the suffering of passionate women,
especially mothers, who defy oppressive societal dictates to indulge
whims of the heart, no matter how fleeting, no matter how damaging.

Even, dearest Hester,
When the finest pictures are hung upon time
With smiles to string year upon year, as if proof

The excavation of the soul does not stop
And the heart you abandoned leaves you worn and pale
Unable to drag the rules you followed

For honor has changed, as all whims do

Godly Lovelessness

Ask Rumi
Why they killed Shamsuddin
Or Romeo. Ask him
Ask Qais and Layla
or Thisbe and Pyramus
Why their world would have none of that
Why not even marriage, time, and children
Could tame the disdain for the fire of Nicholas
    and Alexandra Fyodorovna

But perhaps those are not the best questions
Perhaps questions have no place here
For questions demean the risks taken
The conveniences tossed
The fears abandoned
The courage
The beauty and greatness
Of heeding the urgency of the heart

Mark Antony stirred the world to love Cleopatra
Prince Edward abdicated the throne for Wallis Simpson
Salim fought his mighty father for Anarkali
And Anarkali is entombed alive inside a wall
    to save her beloved
The grief for lost love built the Taj Mahal
And led England to power on which the sun never set

FAMILY

Picture of a Family Man

He works impossible hours
Until the last moment before his children sleep
Then rushes to catch them
And as he carries them to bed
An ache of love overflows in him

Each time he reminds himself
   how precious are these moments
How they fill his heart with purpose and will
It's enough, he tells himself

He might turn to his pretty wife
He loved her once
And he keeps trying to recapture that
So he looks away from the abyss between them
He knows cannot ever close

He touches her and brushes aside
   his yearning for another
Hangs his head in guilt
I have a good life, he insists

But the heart is no fool

He is resigned that his life is not his own
There's a way he already defined himself
A space into which he made himself fit long ago
An image to keep glossy

He makes a list
Of all he has
The perfection of it itemized
Picture-perfect, they say
It's all there, intact and living

This list is long
It's the stuff of envy
What more can I ask?

But it never adds up or fills in
Always a hollowness
A carved-out hole

So he works more
Distract himself more
Polishes the image
Makes more lists
Forces his limbs into the space already defined

But pictures, no matter how pretty
And lists, no matter how long
Are ever only two-dimensional
And a box is no place to fly

Oh Father, My Honor

The great father
Knower of things
Ruler of worlds

He thrusts his will
To thwart the sons
Twice his stature
Half his age
Determined the lives he spawned
Shall exist per his purview
Except when he chooses to loosen the rein

Love, he insists, is child's play
Not worthy of honor
Certainly unworthy for men of honor
And his tribe shall thus be

Honor, of course
Of the sort that can be displayed
Framed

The stuff of society
Codes
Rules
Mores
Dictates

The stuff of norms
Mechanisms
Transactions

The stuff of secret shame
Grinding teeth
Evasions
Distractions
Illusions
And stomach ulcers
Wherein lies flourish, nurtured
By shame and fear
And the heart wilts
Until it ossifies
So the soul is duly
codified
moralized
mechanized
grounded in illusion
distracted

And the sons
Each crippled in a unique way
By paternal love
Are easily now

Quite honorable

How You've Grown

A bundle suckling at my breast
Your sweet breath freed who I am

You climbed my chest
Curled there and slept
And time wrapped us both in a new dawn

The smallness of your hand
Stretched above your head
Wound around my fingers
With all the strength of your needs and fears
And I thanked every angel and every god

When I carried you over that prairie of rubble
I thanked the calluses on my feet

I cherished every mispronounced word
Every new step
Every moment of curiosity
The rocks you collected everywhere
    and stuffed in your pockets
The endless "I love you" cards
The pictures you drew

The songs we sang
The tantrums
The secrets
The sleepless nights
The conversations
The embrace that makes the world a perfect place

Words became small
As you grew big
They've fallen from me
Like leaves from a tree
And land by your feet

In the silence that remains, know
In my chest there is a last beat I'd take
    from my heart for you
In my lungs a last breath I'd give to you

A Wish I Wish for You

Burrow your hands into the sand
    lower your head
    and let the economy
    slide off your back.

Put your ear to the earth
    your skin to your dream
    and peel away the opinions.

Fill your lungs with God
    and turn to let the sun caress
    your beautiful face.

And know
    that my wish for you
    is to live an authentic life.

Sophie's Choice

In those days, when I was defenseless
Small, without my words
Dripping with need of you
With growing limbs I ached to wrap around you
You didn't tell me who I was, Mother
Or that I could dream
Did you just expect?
Or just will who I ought to be?

I know it doesn't show
Because only love can break me
But I can't say it doesn't matter
All heartaches matter
It's how I learned to aspire
To goodness

You knew, didn't you?
The source of that fire
The flaming tongues lapping up your furniture
Strangling the green leaves you cherished
Swallowing the pantyhose without a single run
Coating your new walls with the soot of my innocence

I know you knew
Even before, there was enough for reckoning
And for that and those, his and hers
I always knew you would regret it
Without knowing what you regret
Without knowing it was truly regret
Just a gnawing unease
Karma, God, the Universe, my Higher Self
Knocking at your door
Because life does not grant escape

That's why I kept coming back
To see if the time was then or now or soon
Yet even as I waited
I knew it would be too late
That I could not forgive

And here you are
A graceless specter
Without redemption
Crouching in a maternal vacuum
Accusing even in your pleas

I am unmoved
Cold, as you
But only for you

And now I know what you don't
How it is to become a new person
To wake up and understand that your personality
    has changed
And find rivers running through your body

Yet I was wretchedly senseless
Aligning candidates just right
To stand in that space of choice
Like Sophie's choice, though you are no Sophie
So I can beg and die to be chosen
To cry in my heart, pick me, pick me!
And feel that boot piece my ribs
Refuse against my back
Just to feel the perversity of your love
Or maybe just once to understand
So I might know how it feels
To forgive you

But the time for that has passed
Life planted itself in my womb
And love sang for me

I'm sorry your knock goes unheeded
I'm sorry all that is tender in me becomes stone for you
You waited too long

THE WAY THINGS ARE

Winter

Is this how it feels then?
An exquisite
Fine piercing of the heart?
When grace turns loneliness into a song

The moment you want to board up the windows
And sit by the flickering fire
Trying to see what it is they see and you can't

You search the fire for something
Other than the dimly lit room that you just built
Something beyond the eviscerating orgasm
That shatters on the cold surface of
A body, there beneath you
That you cannot love

In the comfort of solitude
The devastating freedom of owning yourself
Also looks into the fire
For need to burn your skin

But you
Are only calm
Only
Gently blinking

Inheart

In music beats
The ocean meanders
And wanders
And plays
Inheart

Tides of song
And waves of stillness
A ribbon untied

A mockery is made
Of a decision
That is made and remade

It's the heart
The damned heart

Sometimes crazy
Petulant and submissive
Wild and pliant
Unforgiving
But always knowing

Like the ocean
It knows
Never tells or asks

Demands
Come in waves

Where it's just me
And the ocean
Inheart

Insomnia

Something fights against time
And I am the battleground

My wasting body suffers the trampling

Insomnia reigns tonight

Outside the night has spread its wings
Darkness walks the streets

Two blue sleeping pills
Dissolve and cower, useless

Sleep is nowhere to be found
The moon smirks like an arrant thief

The remains of the day litter my thoughts
And exhaustion has curled its roots

But wakefulness is defiant
Only I am more so

So I scoop a bucket of hope from the sink
And splash it on my face

My House

This house is thick with a hushed air
I have not come and stayed here in a long time

The thoughts that inhabit this place
Peer at me with angry eyes
Through the special darkness of its halls

Humors of abandonment slouch
In all of its corners
Like idle hoodlums waiting for me

I am here, aren't I?
Of my own free will
Wandering its corridors
Decorating its walls with words
That make no sense

A tempest that tarries in strange
Rhythms of pointlessness

Lines that dance
To discordant melodies
And feral hisses

To abject confusion
And inconsolable sadness

As I lay in a bed of broken truths
With decaying prose
And words that slit their wrists just to bleed
I think:
I love this haunted place
And I hate it equally

This dungeon of madness
Where my heart
Loves without bounds

I always wonder
If all hearts love this way

This place where I have slain demons
   Where I staged a coup
   To mend a broken bone
   And scrub away bruises

   Where my heart expands beyond expanse
   And I don't care if it bursts

   Where I cry
   Until my skin melts into a pool of melancholy

   Where I manufacture love
   And stitch it to God
   Whether He likes it or not

   Where God promised
   To strike me with lightning

Where I am strongest
Where I am weakest
Where I never forgive
Where I bore a child
Where my womb once cried

This house was built on a lost ocean
I can only get here now on the rafts of memories
Colored snapshots and old movie reels

I scream here
Howl if I need to
This is my house!

Calm yourself
You can hear their echoes
Some are with pain, some fear
Some bliss

Close your eyes and look under the light
That writhing object there is not a snake
But a braid of our bodies, baby
Remember? Look closely
It is a sacred April
Or an April's fool

When you open your eyes,
The smoke of an *argeeleh* will blur them
But I'm not worried. I know you will not stay.
I can't stay either
It's too scary, even for me

But these words are all I have
Maybe all I will ever have

And they will devour me someday
Make a coffin of my heart
To bury me inside
This house

Cancer

She pours her body onto the grass
Limbs stretched and limp
Crushing a world of small invisible lives
    beneath her
Her skin soaking in the dark stillness of the night
Stars shimmering on the surface of her unblinking eyes

Death
Has come to tease her

She doesn't move, as
The long slimy tongue licks her nipples
And parts the folds of her cunt
Death is fisting her

Her heart hurts

It cowers
Averting the foul breath polluting her skin

She doesn't move
Except to close her eyes now

And imagine a pebbled beach
A city of snow
A song she sang out of tune

Just another chance, and

She'll never again take for granted
The wind combing her hair
The majesty of old trees
Rain beating against her roof
Fireflies lighting the night
Freshly brewed coffee and the morning light
Good-fitting blue jeans
Springtime and random smiles
Dogs
Painted toenails and subway performers
Or love.

Lexi

I tried to move life from my core
Through my hands
Into your feet
To your core

Some people can do that
I've heard
So I tried it secretly
As I massaged your feet

How soft they were in my hands
How delicate they had become
These that ran marathons
And skied over mountains

Remember Faherty's?
No, it was "Farty's"
Where the army boys gleamed with sweat
And we watched from the terrace distance
Diet sodas and paninis in hand

I thought we'd laugh about that again
Even when I saw how much time
Had poured from you
I thought there was still more

I thought
If I concentrated enough
I could give you some of my time

Maybe enough that we could make it to Spain
Take that trip to Oxford
Eat lobster until we burst
Drink until the world was healed
Build a playground
Just enough for you to be a mom
Your hair to flow long and golden again
And the shine to climb back into your eyes

I miss you
The tubes and chemicals are gone
But I want you back

Tulips in Winter

Springtime in November
Oh, breathless month

Swept me up
In a warm thrill

A winter surprise
Burned this body

Tulips arose
Through snow

Orange, red, yellow moons
Dancing on a white shroud

Because December came
A reminder

Winter is still winter
Though tulips may dance

New Frontier

Nothing has changed

Time has neither healed nor
Made the heart grow fonder
Love has neither been created nor destroyed

Yet everything is different

I am older now
See the story lines that time has carved
   on my face

The petulant and unruly heart
   has become knowing
And kind as an old friend

I only went to war with myself
Pierced and ripped by my own sword

I held Lexi's hand as she died
Then found her in my dreams

I held and loved a new baby
But it was really Seif in my arms

I bade farewell to Lamia
And she to me, in a knitted bag

I met sweet Yousef
In the regrets at the end of the day

And in her obituary, Wanda
Bequeathed a mother's love

I shredded letters
Then lay in them as if a bed

I burned a book
And wrote with the ashes

I dismantled a story
To know its parts

And there
Just beyond the litter and debris
Was something whole

GLOSSARY OF ARABIC WORDS

adan: the Muslim call to prayer

argeeleh: hookah, smoking pipe

el ghorba: There is no equivalent word in English for this Arabic word; in essence, it means strangeness, or the state of being a stranger. It is used to describe the state of not belonging when living in foreign lands or exile.

fallahat: peasant women

fanoos: Arab-style lantern, used as decorations during the month of Ramadan

fellaheen: peasant farmers

habibi: lover, beloved

jibneh: cheese

junoun: madness

Ramadan: a holy month when Muslims fast from sunrise until sundown daily for a full lunar cycle, approximately thirty days

sanasil: terraced hills

shorabat freika: a kind of soup consumed during Ramadan

souq: market

taboon: underground bread-making oven

wadi: valley

za'atar: crushed thyme with sesame seeds, which
     Palestinians eat with bread and olive oil

zeit: olive oil

ACKNOWLEDGMENTS

Thank you to my dear friend, ma lil bro, Muiz, whose aesthetic vision wrapped this collection in perfect, beautiful ribbons.

Thank you to Helena Cobban and everyone at Just World Books—including Kimberly MacVaugh, Sarah Grey of Grey Editing, and Jane Sickon of Sickon Communications—for turning this collection into the book it became. Thank you to Thom Ward, who helped make these poems tighter, more "muscular" and economical, and to Naomi Shihab Nye, who introduced me to Thom.

I am grateful to "Zoro & Bruce Lee" for my favorite November, and to Majnoun, for my favorite heartbreak. To Natalie, the love of my life; to Palestine, the soil of my heart; and to my countrymen, whose suffering and love know no bounds. To the friendships I treasure: the PfP crew (Sonia Rosen, Hanan Urick, Karen Kovalcik, Abeer Karzoun, Bareeq Barqawi, Jacqueline Berry, and Betsey Piette), Dave Mowrey, Joanne Tomaszewski, Mame Lambeth, Husam Khalil, Ramzy Baroud, Richard Falk, Linda Hanah. To my darling little sister, Lausanne; to Afrika, humanity's beautiful mother. To Gaza's youth, who inspire me—Rana, Sameeha, Ayman, Sarah, Lara, Jehad, Mohammad, Abdurrahman, Ghada, Dima, Aya, Majd, and so many more.

Finally, to you, dear reader: Thank you for being here, with these words that lay bare the world as I feel it.

ABOUT THE
BOOK COVER

Through my involvement over the years with PalFest (the Palestine Literature Festival), I became acquainted with the brilliant design work of Muiz, the artist who creates the festival's visuals. I was very impressed by his work, and even more so when I had the privilege of observing his process. Muiz immerses himself—emotionally, artistically, and intellectually—in the subject before rendering it with visual representation. The results always contain layers of meaning and history that individuals can peel away according to their own experience or knowledge.

When the time came to work on the cover for this book, there was no doubt in my mind that I wanted Muiz for the job. Although writing the poems in this collection was a solitary endeavor, creating this book was very much an artistic collaboration with Muiz, whose brilliant aesthetic sense, combined with his emotional insight into the Palestinian struggle, completed this book.

The cover itself, in my estimation, is a poem. In Muiz's words, it

> uses an emotive visual metaphor to represent Susan's
> debut collection of poetry. The grapevine, resilient,

sweet, colorful, and representative of the wealth of the land and the owner who nurtured it, is here plucked of all its jewel-like fruits. The life cycle of Palestinian produce is so often representative of the Palestinian experience of struggle: bountiful beauty that is often plucked before or just at the cusp of its prime—and yet is destined to bloom with new life once again. The [title] text, spliced above, below, and in between the branches of the plucked vine, also resembles the capillaries of lungs (breath and wind) and the *muqarnas* of classical 'Middle Eastern' architecture, which were emblematic of the relationship between nature and humanity to the grand design of the universe.

This cover was one of several concepts Muiz presented to us at the onset. They all held multiple depths of beauty and meaning. Ultimately, this one spoke to me the most for several reasons.

One of the imperialist colonial tactics Israel employs has been to steal or obliterate Palestinian agricultural land. The social and psychological violence of this cannot be overstated because its consequent toxicity reverberates through time in all directions. Generations of farmers who have tilled the land for centuries suddenly find themselves severed from their inheritance, livelihoods, roots, heritage, and beloved trees. It is an amputation on a society, not unlike a body's loss of limbs. Farmers are then forced into a pool of cheap labor serving Israeli industries where they are often exploited and mistreated.

This severance depletes Palestinian society's ability for self-reliance. Palestinian markets are flooded with Israeli produce and goods—often what Israel discards—and Palestinians quite literally become a captive consumer population with no other options for sustenance than what is sold by their occupiers, who turn the flow of food and water off and on as they please.

The naked grapevine, then, is our society. Depleted, robbed, and weary. But intact. Surviving and waiting. Capable of bearing fruit once more. The formation that holds its sweet fruit is also the airways and capillaries of our lungs through which life is sustained. The poems emerge from, through, and toward the small branches. The breath of our triumphs, failures, and wounds are inhaled and exhaled through its capillaries.

ABOUT

JUST WORLD BOOKS
TIMELY BOOKS FOR CHANGING TIMES

Just World Books was founded in 2010 with the aim of expanding the discourse in the United States and worldwide on vital international issues.

The first titles that JWB published were in the field of diplomacy and public policy, focusing on the Middle East. In 2012, we added a new, more cultural dimension to our list with a memoir by peace activist Miko Peled: *The General's Son: Journey of an Israeli in Palestine*. In early 2013, we published the award-winning cookbook *The Gaza Kitchen: A Palestinian Culinary Journey*, by Laila El-Haddad and Maggie Schmitt.

Just World Books is delighted that Susan Abulhawa's *My Voice Sought the Wind* now further strengthens our cultural presence.

Visit our website to buy additional copies of *My Voice Sought the Wind*, to learn how to make bulk purchases for bookstores or citizen groups, and to learn about the rest of our growing list:

www.justworldbooks.com